Chinook Indians

Suzanne Morgan Williams

Heinemann Library
Chicago, Illinois

J
970.1
W

Photo research by Alan Gottlieb
Printed and bound in the United States by Lake Book Manufacturing, Inc

07 06 05 04 03
10 9 8 7 6 5 4 3 2 1

Library of Congress Cataloging-in-Publication Data
Williams, Suzanne, 1949-
  Chinook Indians / Suzanne Morgan Williams.
      v. cm. -- (Native Americans)
Includes bibliographical references and index.
Contents: The great river -- The first Chinook people -- Living with the land -- Clothes and tools -- Salmon -- Using cedar -- Class and beauty -- The best canoes -- Northwest traders -- Strange traders and explorers -- Living and dying together -- Losing land -- Modern and traditional -- Living Chinook.
  ISBN 1-40340-300-7 (lib. bdg.) -- ISBN 1-40340-507-7 (pbk.)
  1. Chinook Indians--History--Juvenile literature. 2. Chinook Indians--Social life and customs--Juvenile literature. [1. Chinook Indians. 2. Indians of North America--Northwest, Pacific.] I. Title.
II. Native Americans (Heinemann Library (Firm))
  E99.C57 W5 2002
  979.5004'9741--dc21

                    2002006125

Acknowledgments
The author and publisher are grateful to the following for permission to reproduce copyright material: pp. 4, 5 Judy Vander Maten; p. 6 Marilyn Moseley LeMantia/Graphicstock.com; pp. 7, 16, 20 Stark Museum of Art, Orange, Texas; p. 8 MCSUA, University of Washington Libraries, Neg#NA 3995; p. 9 Caroline Ladd Pratt Fund, Portland Art Museum, Oregon; p. 10 Astor, Lenox and Tilden Foundations, General Research Division, New York Public Library; p. 11 Department of Anthropology, Smithsonian Institution, Neg.#77-5712; p. 12 Renee Martin/Weststock; p. 13 MCSUA, University of Washington Libraries, Neg#NA 745; p. 14 Natalie Fobes; p. 15 MCSUA, University of Washington Libraries, Neg#NA 3994; p. 17 MCSUA, University of Washington Libraries, Neg#NA 4016; pp. 18, 28, 30 Tony Johnson; p. 19 Northwestern University Library/Edward S. Curtis's 'The North American Indian': the Photographic Images, 2001/The Library of Congress; p. 21 Courtesy Department of Library Services American Museum of Natural History/photo by Beckett; p. 22 Oregon State Legislative Administration; p. 23 Oregon Historical Society, Neg#ORHI 101540; p. 24 Hudson's Bay Company Archives/Provincial Archives of Canada; p. 25 MCSUA, University of Washington Libraries, Neg#NA 3992; p. 26 Oregon Historical Society, Neg.#CN 014958; p. 27 MGSUC, University of Washington Libraries, Neg#VW 12682; p. 29 Brenda Mosely/Stockpix.com.

Cover photograph by Astor, Lenox and Tilden Foundations, General Research Division, New York Public Library.

Special thanks to Tony A. Johnson for his help in the preparation of this book.

Every effort has been made to contact copyright holders of any material reproduced in this book. Any omissions will be rectified in subsequent printings if notice is given to the publisher.

Some words are shown in bold, **like this.** You can find out what they mean by looking in the glossary.

5/01 A 2422

Contents

The Great River

Seagulls dive. Waves crash. River water pushes through the waves to the sea. Mist hangs over the beach. Nearby, **cedar** and **fir** trees stand 100 feet (30 meters) tall. **Ferns** and bushes tangle under the trees. A sea lion barks.

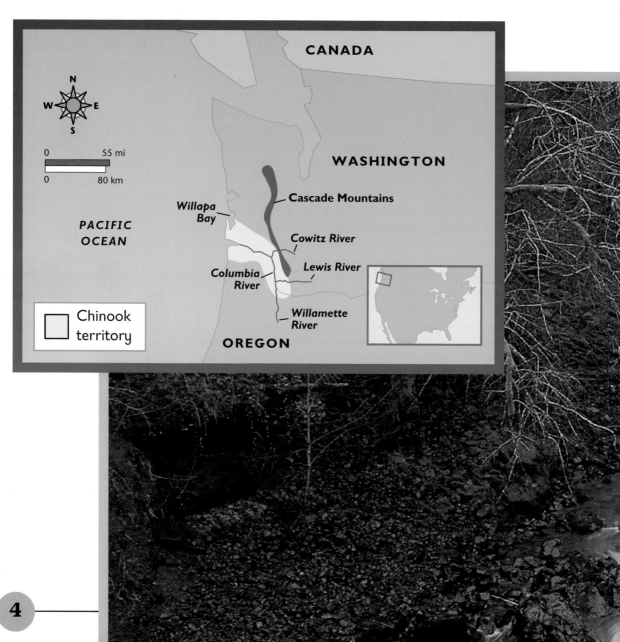

CANADA

N
W · E
S

0   55 mi
0   80 km

WASHINGTON

Cascade Mountains

Willapa Bay

PACIFIC OCEAN

Cowitz River

Columbia River

Lewis River

Chinook territory

Willamette River

OREGON

Here, the Columbia River flows into the Pacific Ocean. It brings water from far-away mountains across a dry **plateau.** Closer to the ocean, rainy weather helps the trees grow. The Columbia stretches wider and wider. Finally, it reaches the sea. Chinook people live here, in present-day Washington and Oregon. They call the river *Imathl*, which means "river" in the Chinook language.

The First Chinook People

Many Chinooks say they came from *Walalawhos,* the Chinook name for Saddle Mountain in Oregon. One story tells how the South Wind caught a whale. A giant, old woman told the South Wind to cut the whale down its back. Instead, the South Wind cut the whale crosswise. Suddenly, the whale changed into a huge **thunderbird.**

Saddle Mountain is now an Oregon state park. Hikers can climb up to the top of the mountain, which is over 3,283 feet (1,000 meters) high.

*These Chinook people have **traditional** face paint on. This 1847 painting was made by Paul Kane.*

The thunderbird flew to Saddle Mountain, near the Columbia River. It made a nest and laid eggs. The giant, old woman found the thunderbird's nest. She rolled the eggs down the mountain. Each egg broke and became a Chinook. That is one story of how the Chinooks came to live by the Columbia.

Living with the Land

Chinooks know they are part of the land and water. The river and forest gave Chinook people the things they needed. Men fished for **salmon** and **sturgeon**. They hunted deer, **elk,** seals, and sea lions. They trained dogs to chase elk. The dogs chased the elk into open fields. Then hunters killed them.

This sketch shows Chinook people fishing for salmon on the Willamette River.

*This bag is an example of Chinook weaving. It is made of **cattails** and a plant called bear grass.*

Chinooks gathered **shellfish.** They caught candlefish, a small, oily fish that tasted good. When candlefish were dried, they would burn like candles! Women gathered berries and roots to eat. One of these roots was *wapato*. Women pounded *wapato* roots into a powder that was used to make cakes. Women also **wove** plants into baskets, mats, and rain hats.

Clothes and Tools

Chinook people did not need many clothes. The weather is not too hot or cold in this area of North America. It rains a lot, so they wore **woven** rain hats. Men and women wore fur **capes** in cold weather. Women wore skirts made from **cattails** or **cedar** bark.

This woman is wearing alikochick, *or dentalia shells, which were used as money.*

*A Chinook craftsperson **carved** this spoon from the horn of a mountain sheep.*

Chinooks wove **nettle** plants into fishing nets. They made many useful things from wood, animal bones, and shells. They made cedar boxes and platters. They made bone spearheads, arrowheads, and fishhooks. They used shells for spoons and decoration. Sharpened shells also made good cutting tools. They used shells called *alikochick,* or **dentalia,** as money.

Salmon

Salmon lay their eggs in clear streams near the Columbia River. The babies swim out to sea. Each year, adult salmon return to lay their own eggs. Chinook people caught salmon with nets, spears, and traps. They dried and saved extra salmon to eat or trade later. Chinooks still fish for salmon. Today they save the extra fish by smoking, canning, or freezing it.

Salmon return to the Columbia River every spring. They can weigh up to 100 pounds (45 kilograms).

*These people are using the **traditional** way of fishing with spears on the Columbia River.*

The first salmon caught each year are treated in a special way. Chinooks hold a First Salmon **Ceremony.** They thank the salmon, carefully cook it, and lay the bones in the river. Chinook people believe that if they respect the salmon, the fish will always return to feed them.

Cedar Homes

Cedar trees grow in the forests of the Pacific Northwest. Chinooks built their houses with thin cedar boards. They lived in villages. Each village had many **longhouses.** Some were more than 100 feet (30 meters) long and 30 feet (9 meters) wide.

Cedar trees grow very tall. They are evergreens, so they stay green all year.

This engraving was made in 1841. It shows what life was like inside a longhouse. The fire was used for heat and for cooking.

Many relatives lived in each longhouse. They slept in special places built along the walls. They could build a fire in the middle, and the smoke rose through a hole in the roof. Many Chinooks spent summers by the Columbia River and winters near Willapa Bay.

Class and Beauty

Each village had a leader. The leader was often from an important, **upper class** family. Chinooks had **slaves.** They were bought or taken from other **tribes** as children. Slaves were usually treated well.

This 1846 painting shows Casanov, an important Chinook leader. Casanov owned eighteen slaves.

This 1860s engraving shows a mother with her child in a cradle board. Chinook people probably did not flatten their heads as much as this engraving shows.

Chinooks flattened their babies' heads. It was beautiful. It also showed that a person was important. Babies were tied into special **cradle boards** until they could walk. A pad or a piece of wood was pressed on the baby's forehead. After many months, the baby's forehead became flat. Slaves were not allowed to flatten their babies' heads. Chinooks **pierced** their ears and noses. Some people decorated their bodies with **tattoos.**

The Best Canoes

The Chinooks made **cedar canoes.** Each canoe started as a big log. Workers shaped the outside first and then **carved** the wood inside. Canoes were less than an inch (25 millimeters) thick in some places. Some canoes were decorated with fancy carvings or shells. The largest canoes held more than 30 people.

Wood shavings pile up inside a canoe as it is carved using **traditional** *Chinook ways.*

This photograph shows Chinook canoes on the lower Columbia River.

The Chinooks used canoes for traveling, trading, and fishing. Sometimes they used canoes for war with other **tribes.** Chinooks often buried people in canoes. The dead person was wrapped and placed in a canoe with many **belongings.** The canoe was raised above the ground in a burial place.

Fine Canoes

"(Chinooks) ought to have credit (for) making the finest canoes, perhaps in the world."

—Patrick Gass, member of the Lewis and Clark expedition, early 1800s

Northwest Traders

Chinooks paddled their **canoes** along the coast, trading with other Indians. They traveled up the Columbia River to the Great **Rapids.** There they met with people from other **tribes** to trade. Chinooks brought *alikochick* shells, or **dentalia,** which were used like money. The Chinooks traded fish, seafood, and dried berry cakes. Tribes that lived far from the ocean traded skins, roots, and basket grasses. Chinooks grew powerful because they were excellent traders.

*This 1847 painting by Paul Kane shows Chinook people drying **salmon** at a trading center on the Columbia River.*

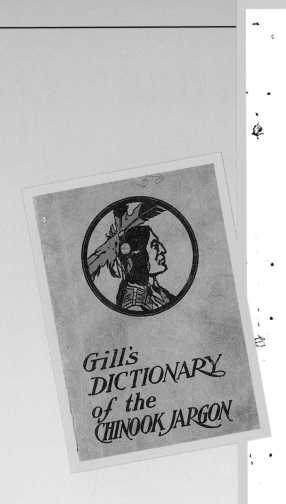

Dictionaries like this one helped European traders communicate with the Chinooks.

When they traded, Indians of the Pacific Northwest often spoke *Chinuk Wawa*, a kind of Chinook **pidgin**. It was easier to speak than the regular Chinook language. White traders also used a simple kind of *Chinuk Wawa*.

Counting in Chinuk Wawa

ixt – one	*taxam* – six
makwst – two	*sinamakwst* – seven
thlun – three	*stuxtkin* – eight
lakit – four	*k'wayts* – nine
qwinam – five	*tathlam* – ten

Strange Traders and Explorers

In the late 1700s, trading ships from New England, Canada, and Europe arrived. The Chinooks traded **sea otter** and beaver furs for things such as cooking pots, metal knives, and fishhooks. Many Chinooks caught new **diseases** such as **malaria** from the visitors. Indians had never had these diseases. Their bodies were not able to fight them. Most Chinooks died.

In 1792, Captain Robert Gray sailed his ship, the Columbia, *into the river Chinooks called* Imathl. *He named the river after his ship.*

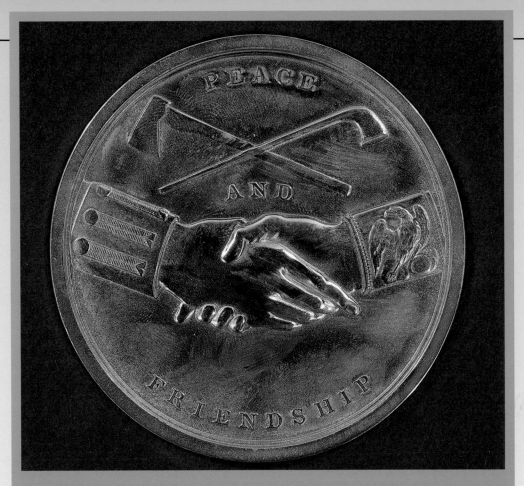

President Jefferson sent medals with Lewis and Clark. They gave the medals to Indians as a sign of friendship.

In 1803, President Thomas Jefferson sent Meriwether Lewis and William Clark to explore the lands west of the Mississippi River. During their travels, they followed the Columbia River to the Pacific Ocean. Lewis and Clark met Chinook people along the river. They spent the winter where the Columbia meets the Pacific Ocean.

Chief Concomly

Some say Chinook leader Chief Concomly met Lewis and Clark wearing a navy jacket. He was a good trader. Chief Concomly is known for protecting Chinooks while helping whites.

Living and Dying Together

American and British fur traders soon followed. They built **trading posts** in the area. Often, Chinooks helped the traders. They brought them food, showed them which plants to eat, and rescued drowning sailors. Chinooks also helped fur traders as guides. The Hudson's Bay Company hired Chief Concomly to guide ships through the dangerous waters at the mouth of the Columbia River.

In 1810, Fort Astoria was built in present-day Oregon.
Settlers *in the fort depended on the Chinooks' help.*

24

SONS.DEL.

*Chief Concomly probably died from **smallpox**. His grave was raised above ground in the **traditional** way.*

Between 1830 and 1834, a **disease** struck Chinook villages. This disease was probably **malaria,** carried by European sailors on the trading ships. There were as many as 20,000 Chinooks in 1828. By 1834, only about 2,000 Chinooks were alive.

Sickness

"Fever broke out...Villages which had from one to two hundred (people) are totally gone. Not a soul remains."
—Doctor David Douglas, 1832

Losing Land

Many **settlers** came to the Columbia River Valley in the 1840s and 1850s. They wanted to build farms on Indian land. They built towns where Chinook villages had been. **Tribes** were asked to sign **treaties,** giving the United States their land. Indians would keep some land, called **reservations.**

As more settlers came to the Northwest, they built towns on Indian lands like the one pictured here.

*As more settlers arrived, factories for canning **salmon** were built along the Columbia River.*

In 1851 the Chinooks signed a **treaty** that said they could stay on their land. But the United States government wanted them to sign a different treaty. The government wanted the Chinooks to move north, near their **traditional** enemies. The Chinooks did not sign the treaty, and they did not move. But the settlers came. The Chinooks lost their land. They did not have a reservation.

Modern and Traditional

Today, about 2,000 Chinooks live near Willapa Bay and the lower Columbia River in Washington and Oregon. Chinook people have jobs and go to school like everyone else in their communities. Many are fishers or **loggers.**

These are some of the traditional tools that Chinooks still use to build canoes.

Chinook children learn about the past by listening to stories.

Many Chinook people are interested in **traditional** ways. Some Chinooks speak *Chinuk Wawa* at home. Some families hold traditional **ceremonies.** They may celebrate naming a baby, a boy's first hunting kill, or a girl growing up. Some ceremonies are **religious.** At traditional celebrations, families invite the community to share their happiness. The family shares food and gifts with the guests.

Living Chinooks

Now there is a dam on the Columbia River. There are fewer **salmon. Logging** companies have cut much of the old forest. Many Indians are allowed to fish, hunt, and gather in **traditional** ways. But the Chinooks cannot do these things. They do not have a **reservation** or the **treaty** rights that many other **tribes** have. Chinook leaders are trying to change that. Chinook people need to hunt and fish in the old ways. They are part of the land and the river. That is what makes them Chinook.

These Chinook men are making a cedar canoe.

Glossary

belonging   something a person owns

canoe   narrow boat pushed along with paddles

cape   piece of clothing without sleeves that covers the top part of the body

carve   cut into a shape with a knife or sharp tool

cattail   tall plant with furry stalks that grows in marshes

cedar   large, brown-barked tree that grows in the Pacific Northwest

ceremony   event that celebrates a special occasion

cradle board   Indian baby carrier

dentalia   long seashells found in the ocean in the Pacific Northwest

disease   sickness

elk   large animal that looks like a deer but is much bigger

fern   plant that grows in shady, wet places

fir   tree with flat needles and hard cones

logger   person who cuts down trees for a living. Loggers work for logging companies.

longhouse   traditional home made of cedar

malaria   serious disease common in hot, wet areas

nettle   weedy plant

pidgin   simple words used to talk to someone who does not speak the same language

pierce   make a small hole

plateau   high, flat land

rapids   fast-moving river water

religious   having to do with spiritual beliefs and practices

reservation   land kept by Indians when they signed treaties

salmon   large fish that returns to the same river where it was born

sea otter   small animal once hunted for its fur

settler   person who makes a home in a new place

shellfish   animal that lives in water and has a shell, such as clams or oysters

slave   person who was bought and sold as a worker

smallpox   serious disease with high fever and rashes

sturgeon   large fish with a snout, or nose, and hard plates on the skin

tattoo   drawing made by putting ink under the skin

thunderbird   powerful, legendary bird

trading post   place where people buy and sell things

traditional   using the old ways

treaty   agreement between governments or groups of people

tribe   group of people who share language, customs, beliefs, and often government

upper class   powerful, rich people or families

weave   lace together threads or other material

More Books to Read

Ansary, Mir Tanim. *Northwest Coast Indians*. Chicago: Heinemann Library, 1999.

Bartok, Mira. *Northwest Coast Indians.* Parsippany, N.J.: Pearson Learning, 1995.

Ross, Pamela. *The Chinook People*. Minnetonka, Minn.: Capstone Press, Incorporated, 1998.

Index